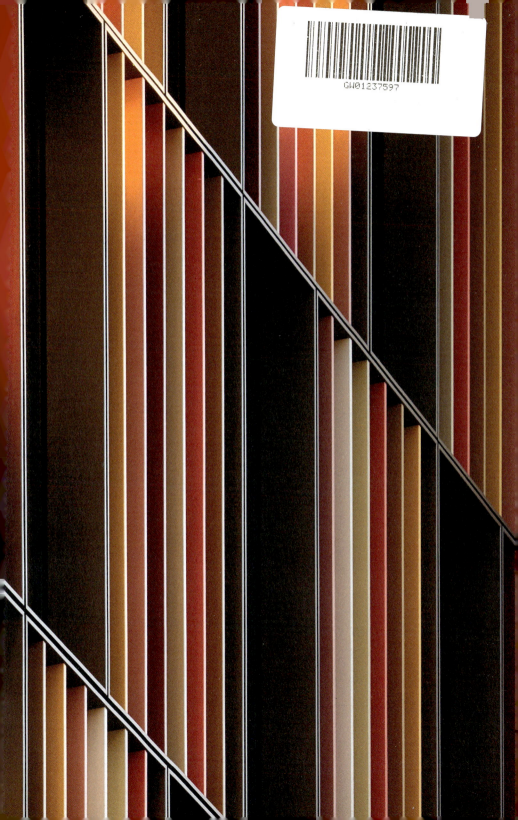

New Scotland Yard
A Minigraph

Allford Hall Monaghan Morris

Craig Mackey

New Scotland Yard is a landmark building that represents over 200 years of organised law and order in the capital city.

Sitting in the heart of Westminster close to our founding location, it allows the Metropolitan Police Service to look forward to the future, and provides excellent facilities and technology for all officers across London.

Allford Hall Monaghan Morris, together with BAM Construction, have brought the old building to life in an innovative and dynamic way. From our public glass pavilion area and our Eternal Flame memorial to the iconic revolving New Scotland Yard sign, the design incorporates the past, present and future of policing in London.

Acting Commissioner, Metropolitan Police Service

Sadiq Khan

The Metropolitan Police Service has been protecting our capital city since 1829, working tirelessly every day to keep Londoners safe. This year, the force steps into a new headquarters, just as a new Commissioner takes the reins.

The new location for New Scotland Yard, which began life as an annexe to the original New Scotland Yard in the 1930s, returns the Met to the heart of Westminster in a slimmed-down, more streamlined, more efficient and better-resourced building fit for the twenty-first century.

It is a fitting home for our world-renowned police service, and I hope it will serve the Met well for many years to come.

Mayor of London

Paul Monaghan

Even before Allford Hall Monaghan Morris won the international competition to design a new headquarters for the Metropolitan Police, we knew this would be an extremely complex project. For example, one of the most important ambitions was to give a sense of transparency and openness – but how do you realise that while meeting the necessarily stringent security needs of a building for a law enforcement institution? Our proposals also had to address the history and traditions of the Met while delivering a headquarters fit for the present and future organisation, rationalising the Met's estate to ensure the best use of public money but also to improve interaction.

While we try to avoid using the word 'iconic', New Scotland Yard was always going to be a landmark building, not just because it's for an important client but due to its very visible location on the Thames Embankment and close to government. We think we've delivered something that reflects both the prominence of that location and the importance of the Met as an institution, and it's been a privilege to be able to do that.

Contents

9 – 30   **Context**
- A short history of the Met
- The Met in London
- Site and context
- William Curtis Green's building
- The client brief

31 – 56   **Design stories**
- Primary moves
- Civic pride
- Public realm
- Public to private
- Open and transparent
- Respectful refurbishment
- History of the building
- Exhibition square
- Eternal Flame and Roll of Honour
- Twenty-first century working environment
- Terraces
- Graphics and colours
- Leaving the lights on
- Flaxman type
- Revolving sign
- Building in the media

57 – 90   **Design in detail**
- Entrance pavilion
- Internal refurbishment
- Facades
- Rooftop pavilion
- Drawings

91 – 113   **Complete**

Context

A short history of the Met

During the first decades of the nineteenth century, a series of parliamentary committees were set up to look at crime and policing in London. Until then, order had been kept by informal patrols and night watches loosely regulated by statutes unchanged since the Norman Conquest. Based on the committees' findings, the Home Secretary, Sir Robert Peel, introduced the Metropolitan Police Act in 1829, proposing the establishment of a new and more comprehensive police service for the capital.

In Peel's view, crime prevention was far preferable to punishment or repression by force, and in a democracy this could only be achieved if the police had a strong ethical code and were fully representative of the general public. In his words 'the police are the public and the public are the police'. His 'Peelian Principles' (which were probably set out formally by the first commissioners of the Met, Charles Rowan and Richard Mayne) are followed to this day, and the legacy of Peel's emphasis on crime prevention is that the Met has taken a pioneering role in the development of new policing techniques and technology ever since.

The service has been involved in many of the most notorious cases in British criminal history, from the unsolved Jack the Ripper murders in 1880s Whitechapel, to the organised gang crimes of the Kray twins during the 1950s and 60s. In many of these cases, the work of the Met has not only prevented further crime but achieved breakthroughs in detection and punishment – which in their turn have led to changes in legislation. George Joseph Smith, the notorious 'brides in the bath' murderer, for example, was captured through pioneering use of forensic evidence when pathologist Sir Bernard Spilsbury ascertained that it was impossible for any of the victims to have drowned accidentally.

1 Sir Robert Peel (1788–1850), former British prime minister and creator of the modern police force

2 The Peelian Principles of 1829, which set out the Met's philosophy of 'policing by consent'

Context

3 1888 engraving of a Metropolitan police officer discovering the body of Mary Ann Nichols, the first victim of Jack the Ripper

4 Reggie and Ronnie Kray, 1960s
5, 6 Daily Mirror front pages covering Dr Crippen and George Joseph Smith

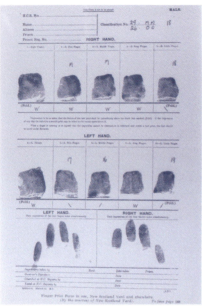
7

8

9

7, 8 Fingerprint record sheet from the New Scotland Yard record office and police officer taking fingerprints, both 1950s

9 The twenty-first century Metropolitan Police Service

Dr Crippen was the first criminal to be captured at sea with the aid of wireless telegraphy. Fleeing to Canada by passenger liner after the murder of his wife, he aroused the suspicion of the ship's captain, who in turn was able to pass this intelligence to the police back in London by the newly-invented telegraph.

During the twentieth century, the Met continued to pioneer new crime fighting techniques – particularly in forensics. The first department for fingerprinting was set up at Scotland Yard in 1901, and in 1905 the Stratton brothers were the first murderers to be convicted on the basis of fingerprint evidence. In 1975, during the 'Spaghetti House siege' in Knightsbridge, the service employed, for the first time, psychological strategies (reinforced through the media) to persuade armed thieves to surrender and release staff who had been kept hostage for six days.

The service continues to be at the forefront of change with the advent of Digital Policing. Significant investment has been made into a technology strategy which will apply information, communications and technology (ICT) in the future fight against crime. These include developing techniques for crime reconstruction (for example, creating highly accurate computer-generated walkthroughs for use in investigations and inquests), and sharing intelligence to counter terrorism.

The Met is now the largest police force in the UK and among the largest in the world, looking after over eight million Londoners across 620 square miles, as well as the millions of commuters and tourists who visit the capital each day.

10

11

12 13

10 1777 engraving of Scotland Yard and part of the Banqueting House
11 Norman Shaw's New Scotland Yard, photographed in 1900
12, 13 1967 view of New Scotland Yard at 10 Broadway, with the iconic revolving sign

Context

The Met in London

Having been tasked to establish the new police force, the first commissioners, Colonel Charles Rowan and Richard Mayne, set up office in 1829 in a private house at 4 Whitehall Place. The house backed onto a courtyard known as Great Scotland Yard. These back premises were soon being used as a police station, and the new Metropolitan Police Service's connection with the Scotland Yard address began. Over the next few years the fledgling Met would take over many of the adjacent properties and outbuildings.

By the 1880s the organisation had far outgrown Great Scotland Yard, and the architect Richard Norman Shaw was commissioned to design a new headquarters on Victoria Embankment. The building was a grand, red-brick Romanesque-style structure overlooking the river, distinctively banded with white Portland stone. It became known as New Scotland Yard to continue the association with the Met's first home. A second, sister building to the north, also with elevations by Shaw, was added as an extension in 1902 and was linked to the original south building by way of a bridge.

By 1935, yet another extension had become necessary, and construction began on a new annexe to the north, this time designed by William Curtis Green. The neoclassical building was completed in 1940. It was occupied by the Met's technology departments before becoming a regional and then territorial policing headquarters, and was occupied by the force right through until 2010.

Meanwhile, the Victorian layout of the Norman Shaw Buildings had become unfit for purpose, and in 1967 the main headquarters was moved to larger and more modern accommodation in an existing office block at 10 Broadway – and the name New Scotland Yard was transitioned also.

14

14 Despite its changes of address, the homes of the Met police have always been within Westminster, the political heart of London. The first was at Great Scotland Yard **a**, and the next in the Norman Shaw Buildings **b**, later extended **c**. The service then moved to 10 Broadway **d**, and has finally settled back on Victoria Embankment at New Scotland Yard **e**

By 2013, however, it was clear that 10 Broadway was no longer efficient in terms of its running costs. As part of a radical strategy which rationalised the Met estate concurrently with changes to the internal working culture and the use of technology, it was decided to return the headquarters of the service to its earlier home in the Curtis Green building (the Norman Shaw Buildings having been appropriated as offices for the House of Commons). For the Met, the refurbishment of the Curtis Green building has therefore enabled a physical return to a historic location, which is now once more known as New Scotland Yard.

15

16

15 Aerial view showing New Scotland Yard during the refurbishment, opposite County Hall and the London Eye
16 Watercolour showing the Victoria Embankment under construction during the 1860s

Site and context

New Scotland Yard sits on the Victoria Embankment, a road and pedestrian promenade along the north bank of the River Thames between the Palace of Westminster and Blackfriars Bridge. Until the 1860s there was no route along the Thames frontage, which was a permeable, tidal landscape of expensive riverside properties and commercial wharves. That changed with the construction of the stone embankment, which reclaimed one hundred metres of land from the river, and protected a new main sewer for the city and an underground line. It was topped with a road and a linear public garden, which was laid out in 1875, and is now home to a series of memorials including the Battle of Britain Monument.

New Scotland Yard occupies a prominent position on the embankment, sitting among a number of Grade I and II listed buildings within the Whitehall Conservation Area, and close to the UNESCO World Heritage Site of the Palace of Westminster and Westminster Abbey. It is at the heart of the government estate, surrounded by ministries and military buildings, and there are high levels of security in the area.

The building falls into a strategic viewing corridor and several protected views. Seen from the South Bank opposite, the building forms part of a great riverfront panorama of historic buildings and memorials, from the gothic revival Palace of Westminster to postmodern Charing Cross Station. It can be seen from Vauxhall upstream to Temple Gardens downstream.

It is also a building with impressive neighbours, sitting in sequence along the north bank of the Thames with Portcullis House, the Norman Shaw Building (formerly New Scotland Yard), the main Ministry of Defence building, and Whitehall Court and the National Liberal Building. This more immediate townscape, and the broader cityscape with its protected views, were important factors in the development of the design.

1578　　　　　　　　　　1682

Context

1746 1834 1872

The Whitehall conservation area lies on the site of the Saxon settlement of Lundenwic, and includes the only surviving building of Whitehall Palace, Inigo Jones' Banqueting House. The neighbourhood is rich in archaeology, with medieval remains lying close below ground or incorporated into later buildings.

Following the 'Great Stink' of 1858, Joseph Bazalgette proposed that rather than existing sewers emptying into the Thames, they should flow into a new main sewer which would be constructed along the low water mark. This would be protected by a stone embankment, and the area behind it infilled.

From left to right: the Aggas Map of **1578**, with Scotland Yard marked top right; the **1682** Morgan Map, again with Scotland Yard marked and Inigo Jones' new Banqueting House; the Rocque Map of **1746**; the **1834** Mogg Map, still with stairs and wharves on the riverfront; and finally an **1872** Stanford Map showing the construction of the new embankment.

17

18

19

20

21

17 River elevation showing New Scotland Yard located between the Norman Shaw Buildings and the Ministry of Defence
18 Portcullis House (Hopkins Architects, 2001)
19 Former New Scotland Yard (Richard Norman Shaw, 1890)
20 The Ministry of Defence Building (E. Vincent Harris, 1951)
21 Whitehall Court and the National Liberal Building (Alfred Waterhouse and Archer & Green, 1885)

22

23

24

25

26

27

22 Architect William Curtis Green (1875 – 1960)
23, 24 The Quaker Meeting House in Croydon (1902)

25, 26, 27 William Curtis Green's work in London: Wolseley House (1922) and the National Westminster Bank (1928), Piccadilly, and The Dorchester (1940)

William Curtis Green's building

The existing Curtis Green building is one of very few in the Whitehall Conservation Area not to be listed. However, it is identified in the conservation area audit as a building of merit, and described as 'a stone fronted neoclassical building which retains its original windows and has a symmetrical composition to the river front'. Its designer, William Curtis Green, was born in the home counties in 1875. He was a reasonably successful architect of his day, becoming a Royal Academician and picking up a series of high profile commissions in the capital. His early projects, such as the Quaker Meeting House in Croydon, are in the Arts and Crafts style but – due in part to their grander scale and context – his buildings of the 1910s and 1920s are far more imposing and often employ a classical idiom. Projects from this period include The Wolseley hotel and the National Westminster Bank, both on Piccadilly. In his later years, he adopted a more austere, stripped back style, as seen at The Dorchester hotel, the Queens Hotel in Leeds and the now-demolished Fortress House on Savile Row – which all provided clear precedents for the Scotland Yard building at Victoria Embankment.

Curtis Green's New Scotland Yard is a neoclassical building in Portland stone, with neat proportions and a symmetrical front elevation. However, the plan is not symmetrical as the building is the only realised part of a larger scheme which was intended to be completed at a future date. Further elements may have been intended to sit on a site to the west (now occupied by Richmond House), the complex of structures enclosing a central courtyard which would have been accessed from a more imposing entrance opposite that of the Ministry of Defence building on Richmond Terrace to the north.

28

29

28 The Curtis Green building under construction in 1940, seen from County Hall

29 Elevation of the original buiding, drawn in 1935

Context

30

31

32

33

30, 31, 32 1960s views of the building in use, showing a car simulator and the forensics department

33 Image from an early site visit in 2013, showing the defensive perimeter wall

34

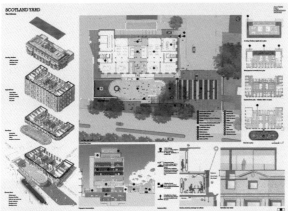

35

36

34, 35, 36 Design competition boards as exhibited at City Hall in 2013

Context

The client brief

The return of the Metropolitan Police Service's headquarters to Victoria Embankment from 10 Broadway is part of ongoing work by the Mayor's Office of Policing and Crime (MOPAC) to improve the Met's efficiency and cut costs, which has been enabled by an increase in mobile technology alongside a change in the working culture.

The £370 million generated from the sale of the outdated former New Scotland Yard, now known as 10 Broadway, has helped modernise and streamline London's police service, saving money, helping keep up officer numbers and equipping them with the latest technology to enable them to be more effective, mobile and accountable. The relocation to the slimmed-down new premises will also save an additional £6 million each year in running costs. Since 2012, MOPAC's work selling outdated and underused buildings has helped to cut costs across the Met and generated receipts of £500 million, to be invested in frontline policing and bringing the service into the twenty-first century.

The competition to find an architect for the refurbishment was managed by the Royal Institute of British Architects (RIBA) during 2013. Following the prequalification stage, a shortlist of five practices was chosen to visit the site and develop design ideas for the building. These were displayed at an exhibition at City Hall in September 2013, which invited the public to give their views. The main objectives were to create modern, flexible and efficient office environments, extend available floor space and facilitate agile working with more interaction between staff.

In October 2013, Allford Hall Monaghan Morris was announced as the winner of the competition.

Design stories

Primary moves

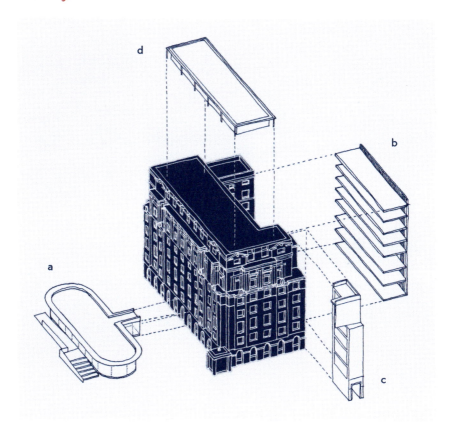

A series of subtle interventions were made to William Curtis Green's building, respectfully renovating and remodelling it to meet the aspirations of the Met's brief. The primary architectural moves were to:

a Create a new entrance pavilion, sitting within improved external space to give the Met a refreshed and more open public face

b Extend the existing floorplates to the west, enclosed by a new facade, to increase the building's capacity and optimise its footprint

c Plug in a new north wing extension to complete the symmetry of the existing building and provide further floor space

d Add a rooftop pavilion, a multi-use space which takes advantage of spectacular views across London

Civic pride

The project presented a great opportunity for the Met to display its civic pride and redefine its relationship with Londoners and London. This is an organisation famous for its pioneering approach to fighting crime in the capital, and its embrace of new technologies to support law and order, so design cues have been taken from the Met's rich history.

It is a project about returning home, and every opportunity has been taken to reinforce the Met's connection with the existing Curtis Green building and to reference its previous homes. The

New Scotland Yard building and address, like its predecessors, is intended to be immediately identifiable with the Met – and its role within the capital.

Public realm

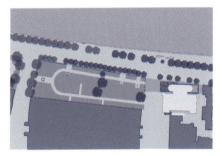

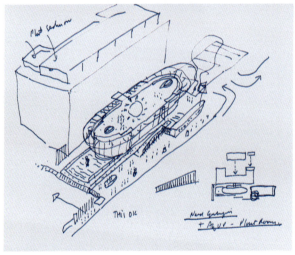

The building now sits in a sculpted landscape for both staff and public to use. This idea was in evidence even in the very early design competition sketches. The Met's front yard is an extension of the existing greenspace of Whitehall Gardens, a public square which celebrates the rich heritage of the organisation.

Design stories

Public to private

The existing building was surrounded by a car park and a high defensive wall. The building now comes to meet the street, the opened-up forecourt protected by a much lower signage wall. Security measures are now designed into the public realm rather than added retrospectively, and take a layered approach combining technical, physical and management measures. The reinstated landscape acts as a buffer, mediating between the public realm of the Embankment and the private spaces within the building. The fluid shift from public to shared to private space helps to discreetly establish the security zoning.

Open and transparent

Core values of the Met are openness, transparency and strong connections with the public. The design reflects these values, both in the arrangement of the external space and the architecture of the building itself with its new windows, outdoor terraces, and glazed entrance and roof pavilions.

Respectful refurbishment

The new architecture draws from the materials, colour and proportions of the surrounding buildings as well as the physical and stylistic features of the Curtis Green building itself. The restrained contemporary architecture of the refurbishment helps to bring the original back to life.

Design stories

History of the building

  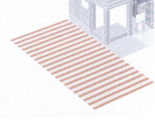

The references to the Met's identity and past begin outside the building, where an 'entrance mat' has been built into the paving to welcome visitors. The stonework quotes the famous brickwork pattern of 'Old' Scotland Yard in the Norman Shaw Buildings next door, and acts as a physical link to the past history of the organisation.

Exhibition square

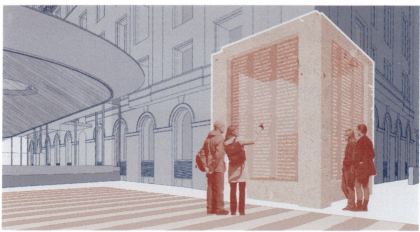

The old Portland stone entrance pavilion in the north-east corner of the existing building has been demolished and rebuilt with new glazing to create a 'vitrine' which will hold a series of changing exhibits from the Met's collection. The forecourt also offers the potential for larger-scale exhibits and displays, such as vintage police cars.

Eternal Flame and Roll of Honour

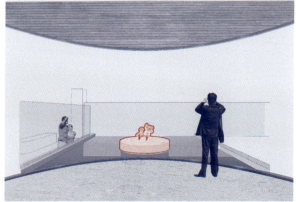

The Eternal Flame honours all those police officers who have died on duty, and was located for several decades inside the hallway of the Met's headquarters at 10 Broadway. It now continues the series of military and civic memorials along Victoria Embankment, and can be accessed freely by the public. The flame sits within a contemplation pool to the south of the entrance pavilion.

The organisation's Roll of Honour, which lists all those members of the Met who have died in service, has been placed in a specially made case in the entrance pavilion, where it overlooks the Eternal Flame. Alongside it is the Book of Remembrance.

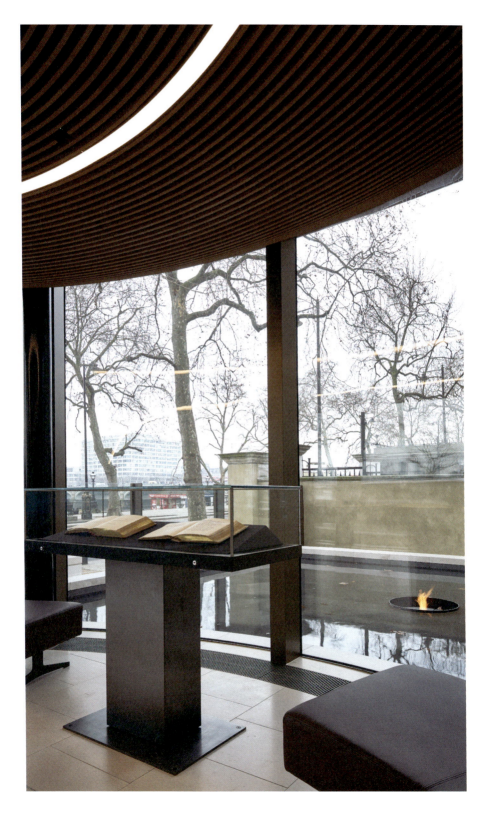

Twenty-first century working environment

Design stories

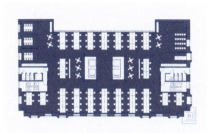

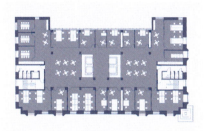

New office spaces have been created by upgrading the historic fabric and introducing flexible open plan working with shared meeting rooms. Greater sustainability has been achieved through smart servicing, high performance facades and flexible floorplates.

Terraces

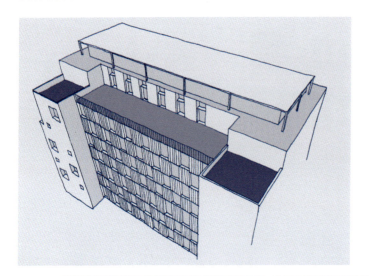

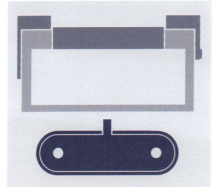

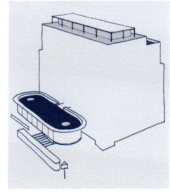

Terraces and rooftop spaces give far-reaching views out across the city. They have a range of uses including corporate or in-house events. Biodiversity in the area is supported by nesting 'boxes' built into the stonework which provide habitats for urban birdlife.

Graphics and colours

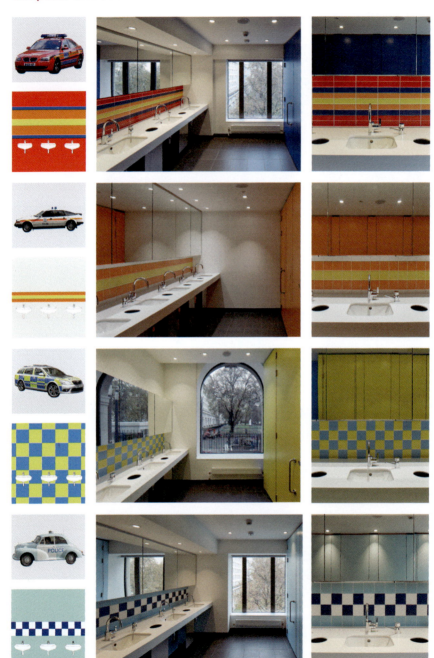

Design stories

The rich graphic heritage of the Met – on its signage, vehicles and elsewhere – is used to reinforce the character and identity of the service throughout the building, even in the toilets and washrooms. The graphic patterns used on vintage police service cars provided plenty of inspiration, and so bathrooms on each of the floors have been designed to reflect the livery of a different vehicle. Bright colours are used on cubicle surrounds and tile splashbacks, against a palette of simple white sanitaryware and Corian counters.

Leaving the lights on

As part of London's famous floodlit Thames riverscape, New Scotland Yard is illuminated at night to highlight the work of the Met to keep Londoners safe around the clock.

The glowing roof pavilion and street level signage effectively act as a modern day 'blue lamp'.

Flaxman type

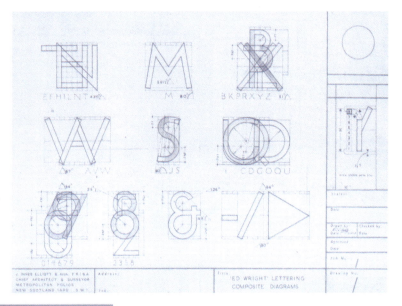

The Flaxman typeface, designed by Edward Wright, is unique to New Scotland Yard, and was used for the signage at 10 Broadway as well as the revolving sign. The typeface, which has no lower case, was inspired by classical inscriptions and was originally transposed from a second-century Roman sarcophagus during the early 1950s. It has once again been integrated into the new building.

Revolving sign

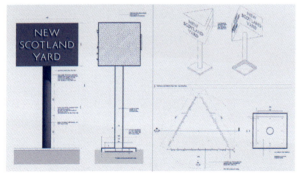

The Met's iconic triangular sign – also designed by Edward Wright – has been relocated to the public square outside the building, where it continues to be one of the most photographed objects in London, revolving around five thousand times each day.

Originally designed for the three-sided plaza outside 10 Broadway, the original concept of the sign was that the 'revolving triangular shape and reflective steel lettering is symbolic of the Met's constant vigilance in guarding our safety'.

Design stories 55

Building in the media

Media reports from New Scotland Yard are immediately identifiable by the backdrop of the revolving sign. The reinstated sign once again defines the setting of outside news broadcasts and inside studio interviews.

Design in detail

Entrance pavilion

The ground-floor pavilion is a semi-public space and the main point of entry into the building. Standing proud of the original facade (and those of other buildings along this stretch of the riverfront), it is the most visible intervention made during the refurbishment, a free-standing object connected to the existing building by a minimal, metal-clad link. Its modernist architectural language helps to dramatise the Met's values of openness, transparency and connection with the public.

The pavilion confidently marks the entrance to the building, re-establishing New Scotland Yard as a standalone headquarters rather than an annexe to other offices. It has an intentionally lightweight construction in contrast with the existing architecture, but sits on a solid Portland stone plinth. Its height and extents are carefully considered in relation to the vertical and horizontal order of the existing building so that, despite differing from it in terms of form and materials, it lines through sympathetically with the facade detailing.

The internal layout is designed to establish a clear entrance sequence depending on the purpose of the visit. Staff are filtered through a security line as they enter, and proceed through into the main building via a rank of three openings in the original east facade. Visitors are directed to a reception desk so they can be cleared for security, and then to a waiting area with curved seating which imitates the geometry of the pavilion and overlooks the contemplation pool. Journalists are filtered to the northern end of the pavilion, where there is access to a discrete briefing and studio suite inside the main building. The press seating area within the pavilion itself can be divided off for broadcast interviews if necessary, the revolving sign outside clearly visible through the glazed walls.

1

2

1 The existing building had very little sense of arrival. Access was by way of a bridge which linked it to the Norman Shaw Buildings, and a small pavilion on the north-east corner which has now been rebuilt as a display vitrine. There was no central door into the building on the east elevation, just a row of arched ground-floor windows overlooking the river. At some point, however, an entrance was punched through and, during renovations in the 1980s, a ramp from the car park in front of the building added.
2 The new pavilion now clearly signals the main entrance to the building on the Victoria Embankment. In plan, it is an elongated oval (known geometrically as a stadium – or discorectangle!) centre-justified in front of the east elevation at ground level.

Design in detail

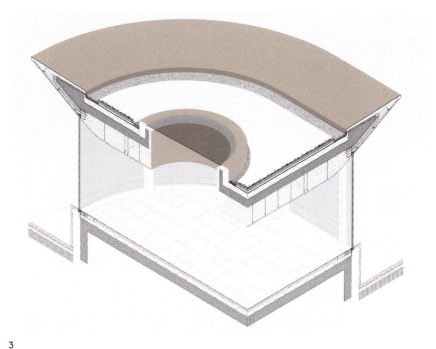

3

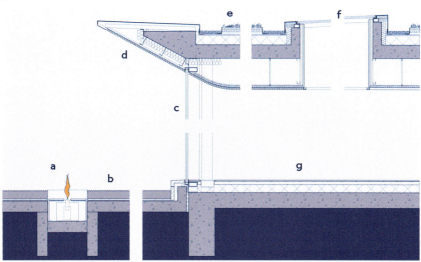

4

3 Cutaway section of the pavilion structure
4 Section through the pavilion and the adjacent contemplation pool. The housing for the Eternal Flame has an infinity edge detail so the flame appears to be floating in a 'hole' scooped out of the tranquil rippling water.

a. Eternal Flame
b. Contemplation pool
c. Glazing panel
d. Timber soffit
e. Green roof
f. Circular rooflight
g. Limestone flooring

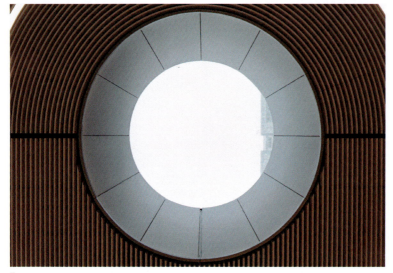

5

6

7

8

5, 6, 7 The structure has full-height structural glazing, chosen to give maximum transparency but effective security. The roof soffit is clad in strips of timber both internally and externally, and overhangs the facade line to provide some solar shading. Inside, the pavilion is circuited by a 'race track' light, which in turn encloses two large circular rooflights which bring in natural light. The bronze cladding panels on the outside are lined through with the stone mouldings on the facade, while inside the proportions of the space also reflect the order of the original.
8 The three entrance-ways are positioned where the windows originally sat, framed in the original Portland stone of the facade. The building's old bronze door bell has been retained in situ as an 'as found'.

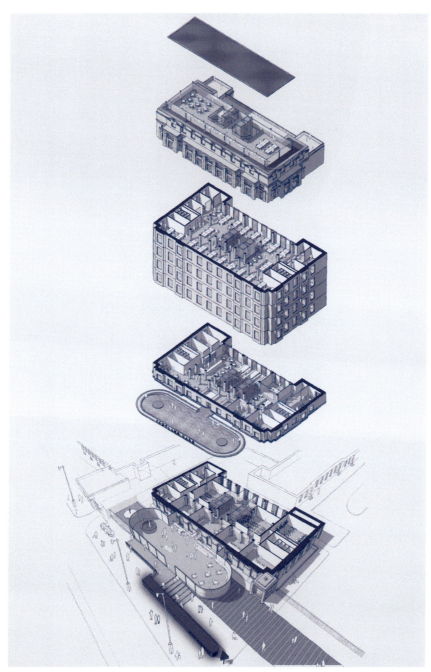

9 Exploded axonometric showing various options for floor layouts within the building

Design in detail

Internal refurbishment

The concept for the refurbishment of the existing building was simple: it should be respectfully renovated and remodelled. From the entrance pavilion, visitors move first into a double-height entrance hall, created by the removal of the floor slab above, containing a number of large-scale graphics and other artworks. A glazed lift sits directly ahead in the centre of the building, offering access to all floors. This again reinforces the entrance sequence which has alternating feelings of compression and openness, from the breezy Embankment into the protective pavilion, through the spacious entrance hall and up inside the building to the view-filled floors above.

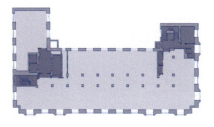

10

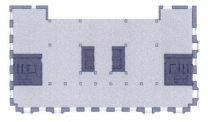

11

10, 11 It seems likely that the asymmetry of the two 'wings' (original plan, left) which project from the west facade was intended by Curtis Green to be resolved at some point in the future, perhaps through the addition of a sister building to the rear.

In the absence of this twin, the symmetry has now been resolved (new plan, right) by plugging a new extension into the north-west corner of the building to complete the neoclassical plan of the original.

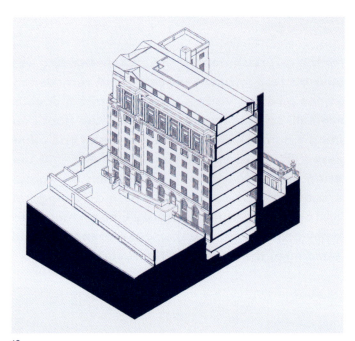
12

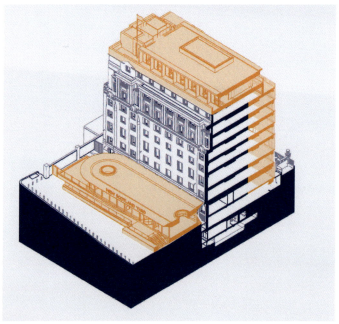
13

12, 13 BIM (Building Information Modelling) models show the interventions to extend and rationalise the internal floorplates.

Design in detail

14

15

16

17

14, 15, 16 The open plan arrangement has been made possible by the removal of many of the structural concrete and steel columns in the original building, with structural integrity now provided by new steel cross-bracing in the north-west extension. Space for the new central core was created by cutting a dramatic void through the existing floorplates.

17 A cut was also made to create the double-height entrance lobby.

18

19

20

18 Three facade treatments: restored Portland stone, new Portland cladding, and the coloured brise soleil to the rear of the building.

19, 20 The original decorative stone features have been cleaned and restored.

Design in detail

Facades

Outside, the Portland stone facades have been retained, cleaned and repaired, and appear much as they did originally; the major change has been to replace the dilapidated existing windows. This move has not only enhanced the condition of the building but also assists with its energy performance and improves security. The new window frames use the original apertures and are doubled-glazed with powder-coated metal frames.

At the rear of the building, the floorplates have been extended out to meet a new facade. Aside from the entrance pavilion, this is the most obvious new intervention made to the original. With Richmond House sitting only a few metres away to the west of the building, this facade gives the office floors vital privacy. The facade system, or brise soleil, helps to shade the west elevation of the building from the sun and is made from extruded aluminium fins in a variety of colours. These pick up on the colour palette of the immediate context and protect a unitised curtain wall system of glazed panels interspersed with solid, bronze-coloured cladding panels.

21

22

23

21, 22 The original windows had small Georgian-style panes, but rather than recreating these in a contemporary material, most of the minor horizontal glazing bars have been removed. Two vertical mullions have been retained which reference the primary mullions in the original but take advantage of the ability of contemporary systems to contain larger panes of glass – and the opportunity for increased natural daylight.

23 Detailed section through windows and retained facade

a Retained stone facade
b New double-glazed window
c Anti-glare blinds
d Raised access floor
e Timber cill

Design in detail

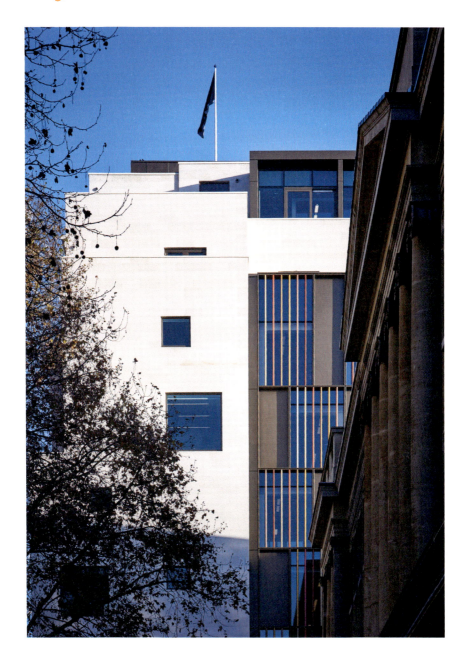

24 The new steel-framed extension is clad with Portland stone which exactly matches the existing facade, but has more stylised, contemporary detailing than the original. The fenestration follows the horizontal rhythm of the older elevations, but is informed in size and shape by the function of the internal spaces.

25

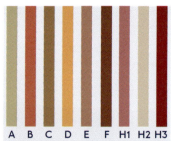

A, C, E
subdued colour
B, D, F
strong colour
H
highlight colours

A B C D E F H1 H2 H3
27

26

28

25, 26, 27, 28 A series of strong and more subdued complimentary colours were chosen for the brise soleil via a pixel swatching process, each tone sampling the material palette of the surrounding buildings and cityscape — a context of stone, brick, lead and copper. These were then matched to RAL numbers for manufacture.

Design in detail

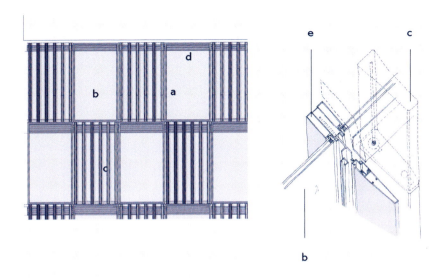

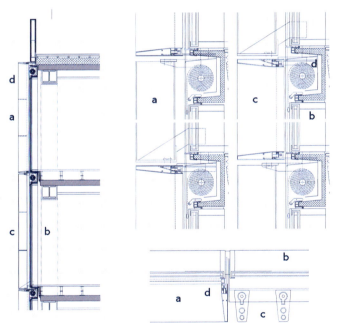

29

29 Sketches and working drawings for an early iteration of the brise soleil.

a. Extruded bronze metal 'picture frame'
b. Glazed curtain wall
c. Brise soleil
d. Integrated solar shading
e. Mullion

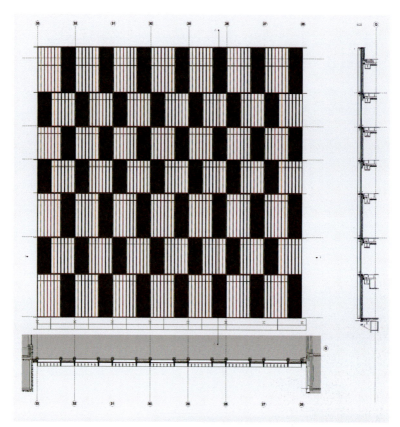

30

31

32

30, 31 Drawings and models were made to develop a tessellating code for weaving the colours across the facade.

32 The coloured aluminium fins await installation on the roof.

33

34

35

33 The form and massing of the roof pavilion draw from the roof language of other Curtis Green buildings, in particular the Queens Hotel in Leeds (1937).
34, 35 Rooftop, before and after. The pavilion expresses the dominant classical orders of the existing building through shifts in the roof height of the pavilion, and in the materials used to define its volume. This central, finned volume is clad in bronze-coloured metal with large areas of glazing, and is flanked by side volumes which house the access cores. These are much more solid in character and are clad in Portland stone with slender slot windows. The stone matches that of the rest of the building except at the cornice, which is marked by a band of much coarser Portland with a high shell content.

Design in detail

Rooftop pavilion

Any rethinking of the roofscape of a central London building – particularly in areas as historically sensitive as this – requires extensive consultation and an iterative process of design. It was essential in the case of New Scotland Yard, due to its prominent position on the river and the need not to compromise the inherent architectural qualities of the building.

In the original building, reception areas were located in the plinth, then the principal office floors made up a 'piano nobile' (principal floor), topped by secondary floors and, above that, an attic floor with a relatively low floor-to-ceiling height. The refurbishment flips this arrangement, placing the principal floors at the top of the building where the views are best, with secondary and tertiary floors below, and the reception – as before – at ground floor level. The rooftop pavilion increases the height of the rooms on the old attic floor and adds a completely new level above them.

On the river elevation, the top floor is set back from a protective stone parapet flush with the facade line of the existing building. This creates a terrace which looks out east across the Thames towards South Bank and the City beyond. To the west, both the pavilion level and the floor below are set back from the facade line of the brise soleil to make another terrace, this time with views across the rooftops of Whitehall.

36

37

36 Curtis Green's original drawing showed two tall flagpoles on the building, emphasising the verticality of the river elevation, and these were included in the original construction. At some point during the 1960s they were removed and replaced with much smaller ones and a radio transmitter.

37 Two twelve-metre poles have now been reinstated in the same location as the originals, topped with blue finials to reflect the historic blue lanterns traditionally placed outside police stations across the capital.

38

39

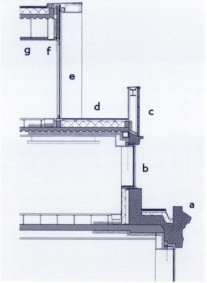
40

38, 39 As construction progressed, rooftop views of nearby landmarks – including the London Eye, Big Ben and the Houses of Parliament – began to open up.

40 Detailed section through roof pavilion and terrace

a Retained façade
b New double-glazed window
c Portland stone parapet extension
d Level 8 east terrace
e Glazed doors to pavilion
f Supply air diffuser
g Timber ceiling

Drawings

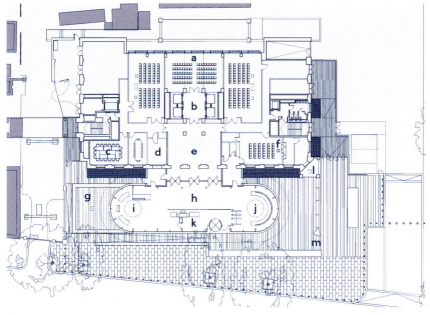

41

41 Ground floor plan

a. Conference room
b. Lift lobby
c. Meeting room
d. Kitchen
e. Entrance lobby
f. Press suite
g. Contemplation pool and Eternal Flame
h. Entrance pavilion
i. Visitor waiting area and reception desk
j. Press/broadcast area
k. Security point
l. Exhibition vitrine
m. Revolving sign

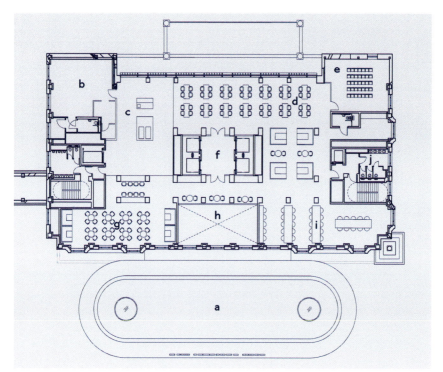

42

42 First floor plan

a. Pavilion roof
b. Kitchen
c. Servery
d. Canteen
e. Meeting room
f. Lift lobby
g. Informal café space
h. Void over entrance lobby
i. Touchdown space
j. WCs

Drawings

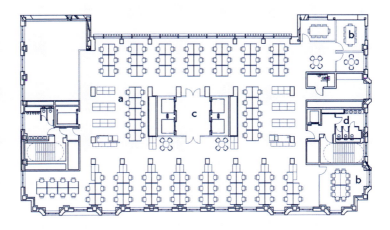

43

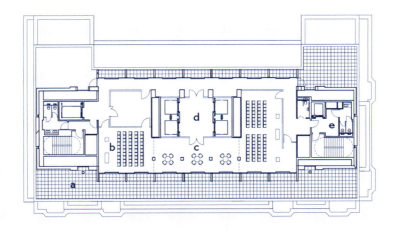

44

43 Typical office floor plan

a. Open plan office
b. Meeting room
c. Lift lobby
d. WCs

44 Eighth floor plan

a. External terrace
b. Lecture space
c. Event space
d. Lift lobby
e. WCs

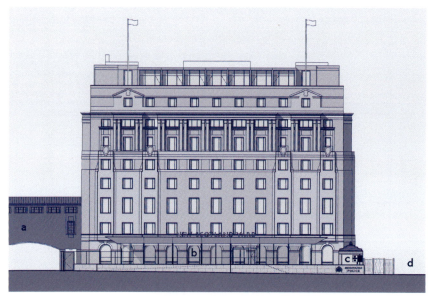

45

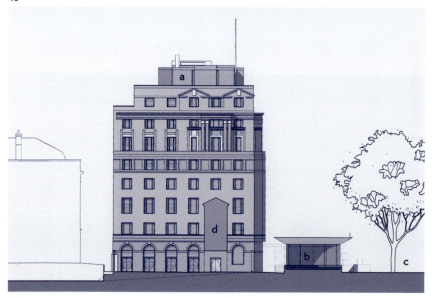

46

45 East elevation

a. Link bridge to Norman Shaw Buildings
b. Entrance pavilion
c. Revolving sign
d. Richmond Terrace

46 South elevation

a. Roof pavilion
b. Entrance pavilion
c. Victoria Embankment
d. Link bridge to Norman Shaw Buildings

Drawings

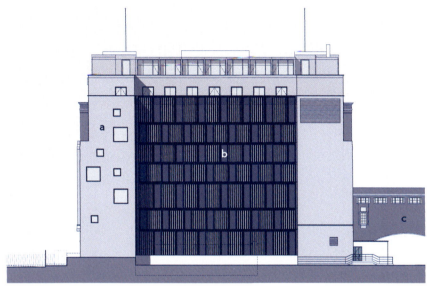

47

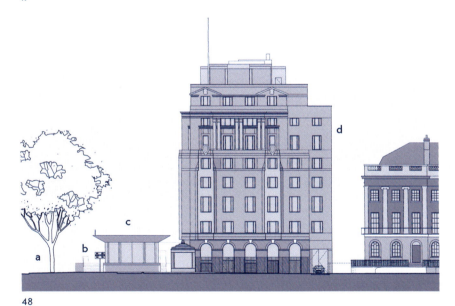

48

47 West elevation

a. New north-west extension
b. Brise soleil cladding to extended floorplates
c. Link bridge to Norman Shaw Buildings

48 North elevation

a. Victoria Embankment
b. Revolving sign
c. Entrance pavilion
d. New north-west extension

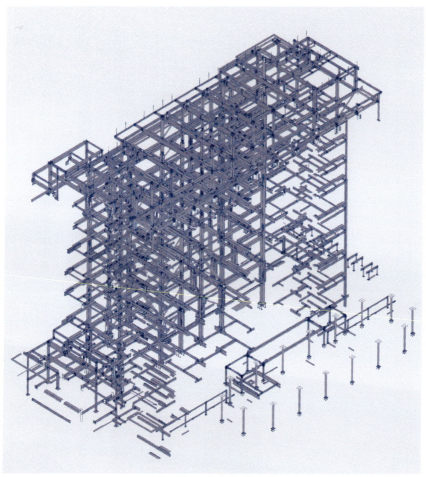

49 BIM (Building Information Modelling) model showing structure

Drawings

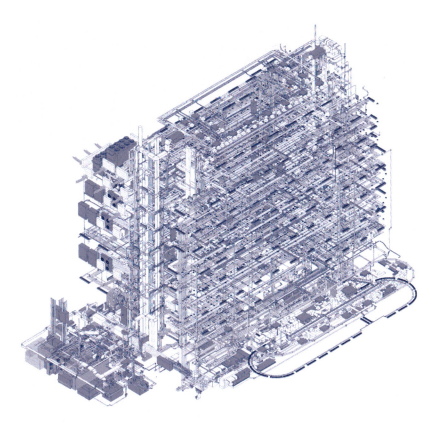

50

50 BIM model showing servicing

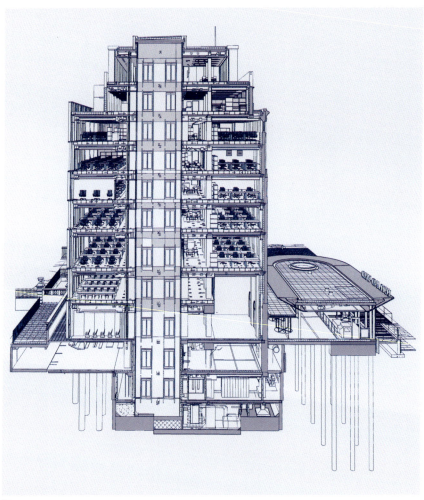

51

51 Perspective section through building and entrance pavilion

Drawings

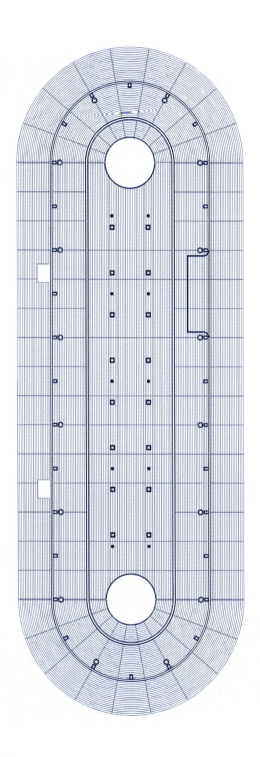

52 Reflected roof plan

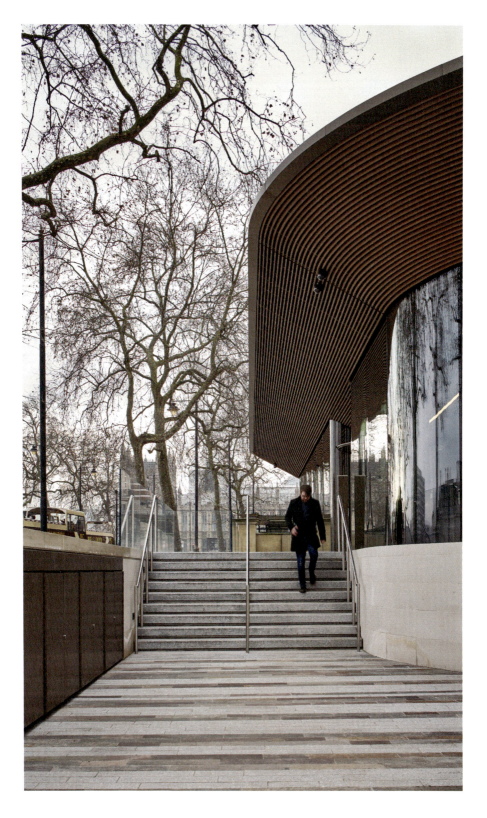

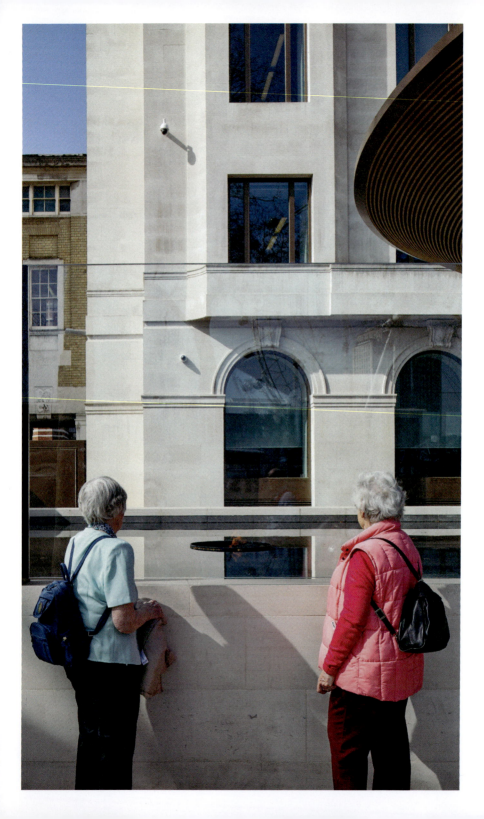

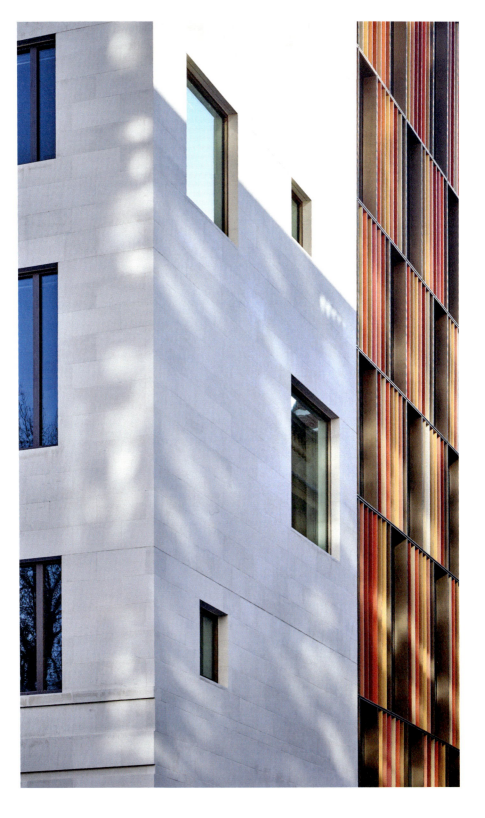

Appendix

Team credits

Client	Metropolitan Police Service (MPS), Mayor's Office for Policing and Crime (MOPAC)
Architect	Allford Hall Monaghan Morris Paul Monaghan, Susan le Good, Simon Allford, Javier Ampuero, Ana Blaya, Micheal Daly, Dominic Dudley, Jonathan Hall, Daniel Lewis, David Lewis, Benjamin Machin, Jennifer Macro, Steven McCloy, Peter Morris, Terry Murphy, Tom Wells, Kirsten Whiteley, Adrian Williams
Space planning	Haverstock
Landscape architect	Gillespies
Project manager/ cost consultant	Arcadis
Principal designer/ main contractor	BAM Construction
Structural/civil engineer	Arup
MEP engineer	Arup/BAMSE
Fire engineer; transport, acoustic and environmental consultant	Arup

Planning consultant	DP9
Daylighting consultant	Gordon Ingram Associates

Facts and figures

Location	London, UK
Construction cost	£65.9 million
Start on site	June 2014
Completion	November 2016
Gross internal area	12,000m^2

Image credits

Cover and endpapers
Timothy Soar

Context

1, 3 Mary Evans Picture Library
4 Pharcide / Mary Evans Picture Library
5, 6 John Frost Newspapers /
Mary Evans Picture Library
7, 8, 13 Metropolitan Police Authority /
Mary Evans Picture Library
9 Daniel Berehulak / Getty Images
10, 16 London Metropolitan Archives /
Metropolitan Prints Collection
11, 22, 25, 29 RIBA Collections
12 Central Press / Stringer
14, 15 BAM Construction
Maps p20-21 MAPCO
18 Janet Hall / RIBA Collections
19 Martin Charles / RIBA Collections
20, 21, 28 London Metropolitan Archives /
LCC Photograph Library
23, 24 with thanks to David Parlett
26, 27 Architectural Press Archive /
RIBA Collections
30, 31, 32 with thanks to the Metropolitan
Police Service

Design stories

p33 Metropolitan Police Authority /
Mary Evans
p39 (bottom) BAM Construction
p50 (bottom right) EyeEm /
Alamy Stock Photo
p51 (bottom) Mayor's Office for Policing
and Crime
p52 (top) Central Lettering Record,
Central Saint Martins, UAL
p52 (bottom) Ed Wright, with digitisation
by Phil Baines, courtesy of the Estate of
Ed Wright
p53 (top left) University of Reading
p53 (bottom) Oli Scarff / Getty Images
p55 (bottom) The Daily Telegraph,
23rd February 2017, Telegraph Media
Group Limited

Design in detail

28 BAM Construction
33 Architectural Press Archive /
RIBA Collections

Completed

p113 Mayor's Office for Policing and Crime

All other photography
by Rob Parrish and Timothy Soar

All drawings, sketches and other photography
by Allford Hall Monaghan Morris

Every effort has been made to trace the
copyright holders for the images used in this
book and we apologise for any inadvertent
errors or omissions. We are very happy to
correct such oversights and incorporate
any necessary changes in future editions.

New Scotland Yard
Copyright © 2017 Allford Hall Monaghan
Morris Ltd, trading as FifthMan

FifthMan,
c/o Allford Hall Monaghan Morris,
Morelands, 5-23 Old Street,
London EC1V 9HL, UK

ISBN 978-0-9934378-4-7

First published in 2017 by FifthMan
This work is subject to copyright.
All rights are reserved, and no part of
this publication may be reproduced or
distributed in any form or by any means,
or stored in a data base or retrieval system,
without the prior written permission of
the author.

Editor: Emma Keyte

013

Published
April 2017

New Scotland Yard
A Minigraph

Author
Allford Hall Monaghan
Morris / Paul Monaghan

ISBN
978-0-9934378-4-7

Photography
Timothy Soar, Rob Parrish

Design
BOB Design

Print & Bookbinding
Bubu

Specification
148 x 217mm, 122pp
Typeset in Granby
Printed on
Peyer Princesse white
X-Per 120gsm
Gmund Colors 12 100gsm
Gmund Colors 54 100gsm
Gmund Colors 35 100gsm
Gmund Colors 27 100gsm

FifthMan